MEN-AT-ARMS SERIES

EDITOR: MARTIN WINDROW

Armies of the Crusades

Text by

TERENCE WISE

Colour plates by

G. A. EMBLETON

OSPREY PUBLISHING LONDON

Published in 1978 by
Osprey Publishing Ltd
Member company of the George Philip Group
59 Grosvenor Street, London W1X 9DA
© Copyright 1978 Osprey Publishing Ltd
Reprinted 1980, 1981, 1982, 1983, 1984, 1985,
1986, 1987 (twice), 1988, 1989

ISBN 0 85045 125 6

The artist gratefully acknowledges the following
sources: an article by Professor Dr Nurhan Atasoy of
Istanbul University, 'Costumes of the Seljuk Turks';
Warrior to Soldier by A. V. B. Norman and
D. Pottinger; *Oriental Armour* by H. Russell Robinson;
European Armour by C. Blair; *Histoire du Costume en
Occident de l'Antiquité a nos Jours* by F. Boucher; *Armour
and Weapons* by P. Martin; *The World of Islam* by
E. J. Grube.

Filmset by BAS Printers Limited, Over Wallop, Hampshire
Printed in Hong Kong through Bookbuilders Ltd

The Armies of Christendom

The Christian armies of the various crusades were not only composed of several nationalities, but were raised by a variety of methods. For example, in the early crusades men of all ranks and from all over Europe took the cross and went to fight Islam as volunteers. Some went out of religious fervour; others, mainly the peasants, to escape the plagues and famine of Europe at the time of the 1st Crusade; and others, mostly warriors, to seize land or a fortune in loot. Such armies carried with them the divisions and frictions of all feudal armies, though they were composed primarily of non-feudal elements; for the warriors usually took an oath of allegiance to one of the great leaders so as to gain his financial support.

By the time of the 3rd Crusade there was less universal religious fervour and the armies were raised and organized by the leading monarchs of Europe on a more feudal basis, with a stiffening of mercenaries. By the 6th Crusade the knights went mainly out of a sense of duty to their barons or the king, or in the hope of gaining return favours, while the infantry was almost entirely mercenary.

Fighting alongside these crusader armies were the armies raised in Outremer (the Holy Land) itself; these were largely feudal, and therefore consisted of the three basic ingredients of all feudal armies: the barons and their retinues of feudal tenants; levies of free men; and mercenaries. Before discussing the Christian armies it is necessary therefore to outline these three basic forms of military service.

A king granted large estates to his barons and the Church in return for which they promised to supply a fixed quota of knights for military service. To raise this quota of knights the barons and Church sub-let parts of their estates to the lesser nobility in exchange for a similar promise of military service. The sub-tenants let farms to freeholders, again in return for military service, and the peasants worked the land under these freeholders. Therefore, each sub-tenant could supply a feudal retinue of at least one knight (himself), with his sons and/or younger

Detail of mail, helmets and weapons from the Maciejowski Bible. The horse trapper (see photo p. 6 also) first appears *c.* 1210; it was in two parts, meeting at the saddle. By *c.* 1225 the fabric was reinforced with plates of metal or horn, and quilted trappers were also in general use by this date. The first plate-metal defence, the headplate or *chanfron*, did not appear until about 1266. (The Pierpont Morgan Library, New York)

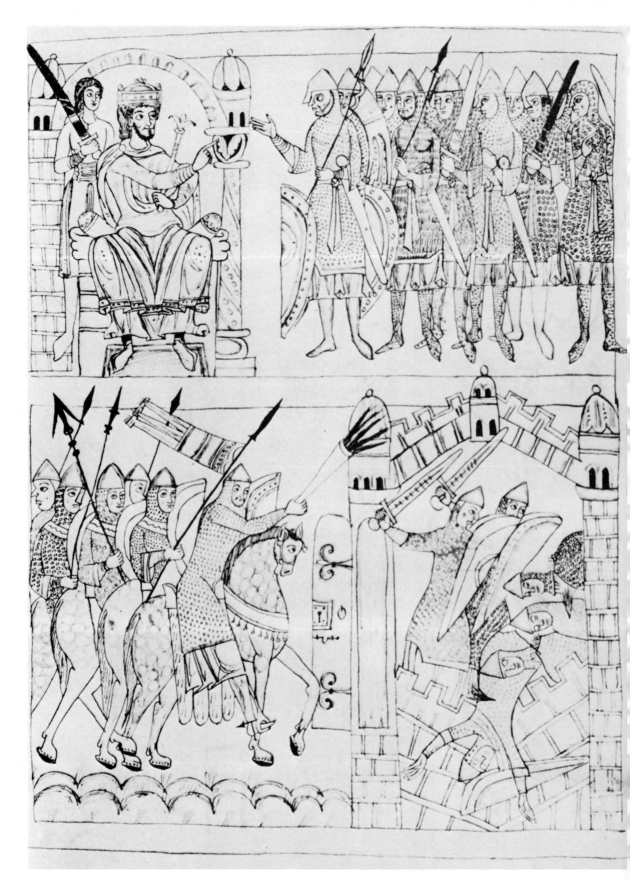

4

brothers as mounted sergeants, who were inferior in rank and equipment to the knight, or squires; the freeholders as well armed infantry; and some peasants as servants and labourers. These retinues combined to make up the quotas of the barons and Church, and the combined quotas made up the army of the kingdom.

The second form of military service, by the free men, was referred to as the feudal levy. The kings of most European countries had the right to summon all able-bodied free men to serve the crown in times of national danger: this force was made up purely of infantry, and by its very nature was neither well equipped nor well trained.

Most kings had also to rely on hired bodies of mercenaries, either to supplement their feudal levies or to provide in their place a professional body of infantry of good quality. The Bretons were well known as mercenaries in the late 11th century, the men of the Low Countries and Aragon by the 13th century, and Richard I employed Italian crossbowmen on the 3rd Crusade.

It is not possible to estimate the true size of the crusading armies which left Europe for the Holy Land, because contemporary sources usually quote vast numbers, which must have been exaggerated, probably including great numbers of non-combatants, such as camp followers, pilgrims, wives and children.

These sources list between 300,000 and 600,000 'crusaders' passing through the Byzantine empire en route for the Holy Land during the 1st Crusade. A figure of 150,000 might perhaps be more accurate. Raymond of Toulouse, who had the largest army, had about 1200 cavalry and 8500 infantry. Godfrey of Bouillon and Robert of Normandy each had approximately 1000 cavalry and 7000 infantry: Bohemond had a slightly smaller following. The total of fighting men was therefore probably not much more than 4500 cavalry and 30,000 foot, the latter figure including all men capable of bearing arms, rather than an organized infantry force. The bulk of the crusading 'armies' must therefore have been non-combatants

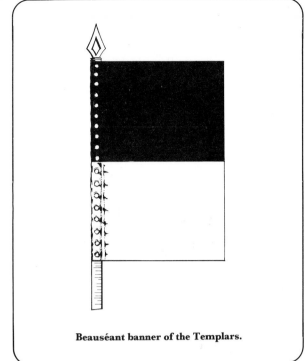

Beauséant banner of the Templars.

at this period. By the time of the siege of Jerusalem (June–July 1099) the fighting force was down to about 1250 knights and 10,000 infantry.

Figures for the later crusades are even more vague. In the 3rd Crusade Richard's army cannot have exceeded 8000 in number, judging by the ships he used. Philip's force was somewhat smaller on arrival in the Holy Land. Frederick Barbarossa's army was by far the largest, possibly 30,000 strong, but only about 1000 fighting men actually reached Acre in 1190 to assist the French and English.

For the 4th Crusade Venice agreed to transport 20,000 foot soldiers, 4500 knights and their horses, and 9000 squires. The force which attacked Constantinople must therefore have been of approximately this strength.

On the 5th Crusade the combined forces of Outremer and the crusaders, mustered for the invasion of Egypt, totalled 5000 knights, 4000 archers and 40,000 'infantry'. Figures for the later crusades are not available.

THE ARMIES OF OUTREMER

A form of feudalism already existed in the Middle East under the Seljuk amirs (see p. 20) and the Frankish nobility simply took the place of the

A scene from a 12th-century representation of the Babylonian wars of Biblical times. The loose gown worn under the hauberk identifies these figures as belonging to the first half of the 12th century; their weapons and armour are typical of those used during the 1st and 2nd Crusades. (Walters Art Gallery, Baltimore)

Turks. There were, however, two important factors which did not occur in European feudalism. Firstly, most of the peasants of Outremer, on whom the nobles depended, were not of the same race or religion as their new overlords; the Christians were outnumbered by Moslems by about five to one within the boundaries of the kingdom. Fortunately for the Franks, the population was not on the whole of a martial nature; some were Greek Orthodox Christians, and served the kingdom willingly. Therefore, so long as the Franks remained strong there was little fear of an uprising; one did occur in the Moslem areas after Hattin in 1187, and precautions were always taken to control cities with large Moslem populations when the garrisons had to be with the field army.

The second factor was the unique position of the King of Jerusalem. The barons had arrived first in the Holy Land, carving out their principalities and counties, and only then *electing* a king from amongst themselves. This restricted the power of the king, with whom the barons ranked as equals. Theoretically the king had suzerainty over all the Frankish states and was entitled to demand the support of their troops, but in practice these 'vassals' could lawfully refuse to give military service if they thought the king was not keeping his oath to respect and maintain their independent rights. Also, the great principalities of Antioch and Tripoli were not part of the kingdom and owed the

An illustration from the early 13th-century Maciejowski Bible, showing the wide range of weapon and armour styles in use simultaneously. Here may be seen the simple *cervelliére*, kettle hat, conical helmet with nasal, and great helm, all in use at the same period. Note also the various styles of sword pommels. (The Pierpont Morgan Library, New York)

king no military service. Therefore, they could only be *invited* to send their forces, and on occasion they chose to remain neutral and even withhold permission for the king's army to march through their lands.

Both these factors seriously weakened the effectiveness of feudalism in Outremer if there was a weak king. But, under a strong king, suzerainty was usually enforced and all states united against Islam.

As in Europe, the knights owing military service in return for grants of land formed the nucleus of the army, but in Outremer their numbers were always limited by the land available. The kingdom consisted of the cities of Jerusalem, Acre and Nablus, with the surrounding countryside. From this land could be granted only four major fiefs (the county of Jaffa, the principality of Galilee, and the lordships of Transjordan and Sidon) and twelve lesser fiefs. The lack of land was compensated for by the introduction of a money fief, wherein a knight was granted a fixed money revenue from a city, town or several villages, in return for an agreed quota of troops. This led to many of the knights owning property in the towns and living there rather than in castles. Thus Jerusalem could supply 61 knights, Nablus 75 and Acre 80. The fiefs of Jaffa, Sidon and Galilee each owed 100 knights, and Transjordan owed 60. It has been estimated

English tomb effigies of the 12th and 13th centuries, illustrating basic changes in the appearance of a knight. Left to right: Geoffrey de Magnaville, Earl of Essex, *c.* 1144; Robert de Vere, Earl of Oxford, d. 1221; a Knight Templar, d. 1250; Richard Wellysburne de Montfort, *c.* 1265. (After Stothard)

that in the late 12th century the kingdom could field a minimum of 647 and a maximum of 675 knights. However, this figure does not include several fiefs lost to the Moslems in the second half of the century, and in the earlier decades the total may have been as high as 700.

Tripoli could supply a further 100 knights; Edessa about the same number. Antioch had about the same total of knights as Jerusalem.

The Church in Palestine was immensely rich in lands, property and money fiefs and also had to supply many soldiers for service to the king, as had some of the larger urban communities. These troops are usually referred to as 'sergeants', though in some cases they appear to have been in fact city militia. Their first duty was always the defence of their own cities and surrounding countryside but contingents were called upon to serve in the field army of the kingdom in times of emergency, and they can therefore be regarded as reservists whose training and equipment were inferior to those of the knights and the mercenary foot soldiers.

Some of the known quotas for sergeants were: the

Although rarely mentioned, the Phrygian-shaped helmet of the Saxons constantly appears in manuscripts of the 11th and 12th centuries. In this example, from Angoulême Cathedral and dated *c.* 1128, the bottom edge at the rear is extended to protect the neck. Such helmets appear in illuminated manuscripts and sculptures as late as *c.* 1218.

Patriarch of Jerusalem, the Chapter of the Holy Sepulchre, and the cities of Jerusalem and Acre, 500 sergeants each; Nablus, 300; the bishop of Bethlehem, 200; the abbot of Mount Sion, the archbishops of Nazareth and Tyre, the bishop of Acre, and the port of Ascalon, 150 each; the ports of Jaffa and Tyre, 100 each; the ports of Arsuf and Caesarea, 50 each. Edessa supplied a further 700 sergeants and by about 1180 there were an estimated 5025 sergeants available to the kingdom. Antioch had another 3000 in the early 12th century.

The able-bodied population of the kingdom of Jerusalem, including the native Christian Syrians, could also be called out as the feudal levy in emergencies, for example to repel the large scale invasion by Saladin in 1187. However, such levies appear to have been called out principally to supply manpower, not fighting power, and this is borne out by the fact that many of the known levies were used to besiege towns, or for the rapid construction of castles in the immediate vicinity of the enemy.

In Antioch and Edessa the native peoples were noted for their warlike qualities, and both principality and county could field levies of Armenian cavalry and infantry which were of a reasonable quality.

During the 12th century the Moslems grew stronger through unity, while the Franks were unable to increase their manpower, and in fact diminished in strength when Edessa, and the considerable fighting force it supported, was lost in mid-century. The obvious answer to the manpower problem was the hiring of mercenaries but the large percentage of the kingdom's revenue taken by the Italians, through concessions granted to them in the early years for assistance rendered, prevented the kingdom from ever being able to afford all the mercenaries it needed.

Some mercenaries were employed by the kingdom during the first half of the 12th century but in the second half the kingdom became more and more dependent on these mercenaries to keep up the strength of the army. From 1183 a tax had to be levied to pay these troops, and the kings of Europe frequently sent money to buy the services of mercenaries rather than lead their own armies on the dangerous march overland to the Holy Land.

Mercenaries were mainly employed to provide a reliable infantry arm for the army, although some knights were also hired. Armed with crossbow or spear, the infantry's main functions were to repulse any mounted attacks by presenting a hedge of spear points; to provide the missile factor; and to provide a firm base from the cover of which the knights could charge, or behind which they could rally between charges. The crossbowmen played a particularly important role, frequently being stationed at the front and/or wings of the battle line, and almost all battles of the late 12th and 13th centuries in the Middle East mention the good service given by the crossbowmen. It is notable that at Mansourah in 1250, for example, Louis IX considered his position extremely hazardous until he could get his corps of crossbowmen across the river to support his cavalry.

A light cavalry arm was supplied by the Turcopoles, who were mercenaries recruited from the native Syrians and were the offspring of mixed marriages between the lower classes of Franks and Syrians. Some of these troops used the bow, and appear to have followed the Turkish method of fighting as mounted bowmen with hit-and-run tactics, but this was probably only when employed for reconnaissance and screening duties, and their real role was to bolster the number of knights, with whom they normally rode, by forming a second line of cavalry.

Organization

The armies of Outremer were organized at the muster for each campaign according to the task that lay ahead and there was no permanent organization as such. However, it was customary to divide most medieval armies into a number of divisions, and in Outremer each division was allotted a specific task and given strict orders so that the commander-in-chief could maintain control over all the divisions on a battlefield for as long as possible. This was vital if the Turkish tactics, of attempting to break up the crusaders' formations with lightning missile attacks from all directions, were to be defeated. Great attention was therefore paid to the allotting of positions and the maintenance of rigid, tight-knit lines. This rigidity of formation was not abandoned until the decisive charge of the heavy cavalry was launched, after which the commander-in-chief in any case lost overall control. Frequently the infantry was deployed in front of the cavalry to protect the horses of the knights, enduring the Turks' barrage of arrows but suffering little damage, until the right

A brass from a reliquary case or similar, dated 12th or early 13th century and probably made at Limoges. This illustrates the general appearance of many knights until the 3rd Crusade, and most spearmen (without the long gown, shown here under the hauberk) until about 1225. (Reproduction by permission of the Trustees of the Wallace Collection)

9

moment came for the cavalry to charge.

Because of the Turks' tactics of harassing any force on the move, without committing themselves to a full scale battle, special attention was also paid to the formation of units on the march, with van, rear and flank guards playing an important role. Archers and crossbowmen were usually predominant in these divisions.

Too little credit is given to this aspect of organization and discipline in the Outremer armies; their history is studded with examples of their maintenance of rigid formation whilst marching through the enemy. On these occasions the foot soldiers marched on the outside of the cavalry so as to shield the knights' precious horses from the arrows of the Turkish horsemen.

Generally speaking the men were placed under the command of their own lords within these divisions, and the tasks of vanguard, rearguard and

A great helm of the mid-13th century. Note reinforcing strips at eye slits and down the front to form a cross, and angled front to deflect blows. Such helmets weighed between 15 and 20 lbs.

reserve were allotted to those contingents whose make-up was most suited to the role. The spearmen and archers were organized in small companies or bands; the knights were divided into groups of between 20 and 25 men on average, again mostly following the banner of their overlord. The reserve was usually commanded by the commander-in-chief and was used to reinforce any threatened point or to prevent attack from the rear by the highly mobile Turks.

A particularly effective formation used by the crusaders on the march in 1099 and again in 1119 was a division of nine 'squadrons' of knights in three ranks of three 'squadrons', which formed a cavalry square capable of meeting an attack from any direction. This formation was only suitable for open country, however, and in the broken terrain of Syria the army more usually marched in a long column.

The chief military officer of the kingdom was the Constable, who was responsible for military supplies and justice, and the hiring and control of mercenaries. If the king was absent from an expedition, the Constable became commander-in-chief; his lieutenant was the Marshal. Both the Hospitallers and Templars provided military advisers who were highly valued for their experience of war in the Holy Land, but the two orders were often at loggerheads in the 13th century and this made for disunity and several drastic decisions which cost the kingdom many worthy knights it could ill afford to lose.

However, in general the commanders of the armies of Outremer were hard-headed, practical fighting men, who proved able to adapt their methods of warfare to meet new weapons and tactics. As any defeat could spell utter disaster, many campaigns were entirely campaigns of manoeuvre; the annual Seljuk invasions between 1110 and 1115, for example, were all cancelled out by manoeuvre alone. In 1115 the knights and feudal levies were kept in the field all summer before the Turks were decisively defeated at the battle of Tell Danith. But the importance of that battle fades into insignificance beside the fact that, in an age when the armies of Europe could rarely be held in the field for more than six to eight weeks, the army of Outremer remained in the field for five months.

Logistics

The art of logistics had practically disappeared in western Europe after the fall of the western half of the Roman Empire, and the European armies of the Middle Ages lived mainly off the land. However, in the semi-arid lands of the Middle East, with long marches over dry and barren land, on campaigns lasting far longer than in the West, the Franks had to learn the art or die. In the 1st and 2nd Crusades thousands of crusaders did die of starvation and thirst—in fact more were lost this way than from any other single cause—but by the time of the 3rd Crusade the leaders, at least, had learnt their lesson. Frederick Barbarossa insisted that every German crusader should have sufficient money to keep himself and his family abroad for a year. Diplomats were sent ahead of the three armies to arrange safe passage and the purchasing of supplies, and Richard in particular showed a keen grasp of logistics by establishing a supply base at Cyprus.

The armies of Outremer itself soon learnt that their basic role of defending the Holy Land against attack meant that a series of well-supplied bases beside the main water sources were needed, at which the field army could camp for some time in order to deny the Saracens water. When necessary, supply columns were also organized, but they do not seem to have been as fully developed as those of the Moslems.

There was little in the way of medical care, and, judging by the examples of medical treatment quoted in contemporary sources, it would appear that a man was better off without medical attention. Some barons employed skilled Moslem doctors in their households but this does not mean that these doctors would have served their master's soldiers in the field.

THE MILITARY ORDERS

After Jerusalem was captured in 1099, most of the crusaders returned to Europe and only some 300 knights remained to defend the newly won kingdom. There were smaller forces at Edessa and Antioch, but here the new princes were busy consolidating and expanding their new principalities. The problem was how to defend the kingdom with such a small force.

A 12th-century sculpture of a Norman knight. He wears a short-sleeved hauberk with attached coif, and the simple conical helmet without nasal piece. The shield protects his left side, his right being defended by his weapon.

Early in the 12th century a partial answer was supplied by small bands of crusaders who, out of religious devotion, voluntarily dedicated themselves to protecting the pilgrims en route to the Holy Land. Before long the Church recognized the worth of these men and accepted them as part of its own establishment, soldier-monks of noble birth who took vows of poverty, chastity and obedience and wore monks' habits in the chapel, but who also rode to battle in mail and the distinctive cloak or surcoat of their order; they were professional soldiers ruled by an iron discipline and they formed the famous military orders.

By the 1140s one such order, the Templars, were playing an important role in the military defence of the kingdom, and after mid-century contingents of the Templars and Hospitallers formed a large part of the royal army in the field. Recruits and money flowed into these two great orders and by the last quarter of the century they were the chief land owners in Outremer, their knights were entrusted with the safe keeping of the greatest and most important castles in the land, and the network of communications in the Holy Land was policed by their patrols. By the early 13th century their knights, sergeants and hired mercenaries formed approximately half of any field army.

The precise number of soldiers supplied by the military orders is unknown. For the Egyptian campaign of 1158 the Hospitallers contributed 500 knights. Each knight was usually accompanied by two squires who were non-combatants. However, there would have been at least equal numbers of sergeants and Turcopole mercenaries, so a total of 2000 would not be unreasonable. The Templars agreed to supply 500 knights and 500 Turcopoles to assist King Amalric (1163–74) in return for grants of land. By mid-13th century the Templars and Hospitallers could field only between 200 and 300 knights each, although a small number must have remained in the various castles and should be added to the total strength.

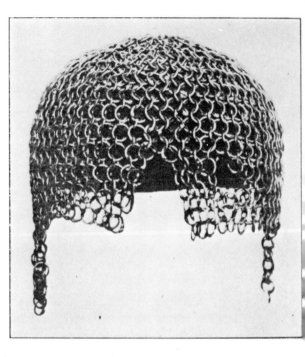

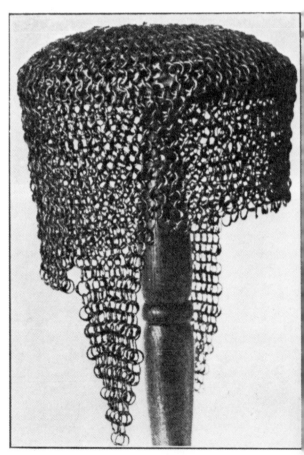

Two mail coifs attributed to the 13th or 14th century. Their origins and date are suspect, but they do serve to illustrate the form of separate coifs in the crusading era.

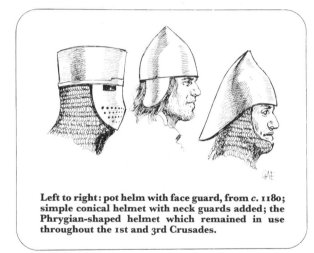

Left to right: pot helm with face guard, from *c.* 1180; simple conical helmet with neck guards added; the Phrygian-shaped helmet which remained in use throughout the 1st and 3rd Crusades.

The Knights of the Temple was the first of the military orders, formed in 1118 by seven knights who swore to protect pilgrims and observe monastic vows. The order was recognized by the Pope in 1128 as a branch of the Cistercian Order and in 1147 fought its first major action against the Saracens.

In 1145 the Knights Templar were granted permission to wear the white hooded mantle of the Cistercians: this was replaced by a white cloak on active service and from the time of the 2nd Crusade a red cross was worn on the left breast and on the shield. Sergeants wore a brown mantle or cloak. Lance pennons were also white, with the cross of the order, and the banner was black and white.

The Order of the Knights of St John of Jerusalem, or the Hospitallers, was originally founded in 1070 as a purely hospitaller order for the succour of pilgrims in the Holy Land, but by the end of the first quarter of the 12th century there appears to have been some form of military organization developing, possibly only a constable and one or two officers responsible for paying and controlling mercenaries to defend the order's possessions. Between 1136 and 1142 the order received as gifts a number of key fortresses and, by 1157 at the latest, was engaged in warfare, not just defending its possessions. In 1168 it was able to send 500 knights on the invasion of Egypt, which suggests that by mid-century it was fulfilling a military as well as hospitaller role.

The Pope granted the order a red banner with a white cross in 1130; sometime between 1120 and 1160 it was laid down that a white cross should be worn on the black mantle of the St Augustine Order, of which the Hospitallers were a branch. The cross was probably a plain Latin one until the mid-13th century. In 1248 the mantle was replaced by a black surcoat with the white cross on the breast, but in 1259 this was changed to a red surcoat.

The third major military order in the Holy Land was the Teutonic Order, founded as a hospitaller order following the Cistercian rule during the siege of Acre in 1189–90. The order was recognized by the Pope in 1191 and in 1198 became a military order. As the Templars and Hospitallers were already well established in Syria, the Teutonic Knights concentrated on the Antioch and Tripoli regions, but in 1210 most of the knights and their Hochmeister were killed. A new headquarters was then established near Acre, but the Teutonic Knights were always overshadowed by the other two orders in the Holy Land and their real greatness was founded in northern Europe.

In 1230 twenty knights and 200 sergeants were sent to Prussia to convert the pagan tribes to Christianity and by 1237 had succeeded in reducing all resistance and had begun to colonize the region. The Order then moved into Livonia but in 1242 the Prussian tribes rebelled and a crusade of 60,000 Germans and Bohemians was launched to save the Order and its conquests. The territories were under full control again by 1260 and the

Face and reverse of a pair of poleyns, attributed to the mid-13th century. Again, the date is suspect, but these illustrations do show details not normally visible in other sources, eg, the ribbing to strengthen the plate and the manner in which the mail of the *chausses* was attached at top and bottom. The rivets at the sides may also have helped secure the poleyns to the mail.

Tomb effigy of Don Bernaldo Guillen de Entenza (d. 1237), one of the leading knights of Jaime I of Aragon. The greaves are unusual at this date: they do not usually appear until *c.* 1300. However, the Spanish were at this date a close second to the Italians as leaders of military fashion; by 1257 they had established an armourers' guild at Barcelona. It is possible therefore that greaves were in use by the nobles in the second half of the century.

Order then moved into Samaiten and Courland to unite Livonia and Prussia. These lands were conquered by 1267, only for the Order to be confronted by another Prussian revolt which was not crushed until 1280.

The Teutonic Knights wore a white cloak or surcoat with a black Latin cross from about 1191; the sergeants wore a grey cloak or surcoat with a truncated cross, ie, without the vertical section of the stem above the horizontal arms.

Another purely German military order, founded in 1204 by the bishop of Riga to protect the German colonists of that city, was the Brethren of the Sword. By 1206 the order had about 50 knights, but a third of these were killed between 1212 and 1223 and over half the Order's members were killed in 1237. The survivors then united with the Teutonic Order in Livonia, although they remained independent of the Teutonic Hochmeister.

In Iberia the armies of the various Spanish and Portuguese kindoms, always short of manpower as they regained vast tracts of land from the Moors, were heavily reinforced by a number of military orders. Originally the Templars and Hospitallers had been given lands and castles to hold for the kings, but neither of these orders was prepared to commit themselves heavily in Iberia and between about 1160 and 1170 several Spanish military orders sprang up to take their place, most originating from small bands or associations of knights who held frontier fortresses. The major orders were Calatrava and Santiago.

The Knights of Calatrava was the first Spanish order to be formed, in 1157, when a group of Cistercian monks and Navarrese soldiers agreed to hold the strategic castle of Calatrava (guarding the road to Toledo), which had been abandoned by the Templars. By the end of 1158 these men had cleared the surrounding area of Moorish raiders. The monks returned to their abbey in 1164 and in the same year the military section remaining at the castle was recognized as a military order by the Pope.

The knights originally wore the white hooded mantle of the Cistercians but the surcoat was soon adopted for active service. No insignia was worn and the knights' armour was always painted black.

The Knights of Santiago originated from a band of thirteen knights who protected pilgrims travelling to the shrine of St James at Compostella during the period 1158–64. In 1175 the knights were recognized as a military order by the Pope. They wore a white habit with a red cross on the left breast; the bottom arm of the cross resembled a sword blade. The Portuguese branch of the order, Sao Thiago, also wore a white habit and red cross but the bottom arm of their cross ended in a fleur-de-lis.

In 1162 there existed a small group of Portuguese knights known as the Brethren of Santa Maria. In 1170 they adopted the Benedictine rule. After the Moorish attacks on Portugal in 1190 the order built many posts north of the Tagus and in 1211 acquired the town of Aviz, becoming known then as the Knights of Aviz. The knights probably wore a black cloak or surcoat, being of the Benedictine rule.

Around 1166 another group of knights, known as the Knights of St Julian, was operating on the Castile and Leon frontier. They were recognized as a military order by the Pope in 1183. By 1264 there were 600 knights and 2000 sergeants. They wore a white cloak or surcoat.

The Knights of Our Lady of Montjoie were founded by a former knight of Santiago about 1176 in the Holy Land, and were recognized by the Pope in 1180. A small detachment fought at Hattin, after which most of the Order retired to Aragon and were incorporated with Calatrava in 1221. The knights wore a white habit with a red and white cross, the form of which is unknown.

THE IBERIAN ARMIES

Until the 11th century most of the fighting between the Moors and the small Christian kingdoms of Iberia was confined to the mountainous regions north of the Douro, and therefore the infantry was the dominant arm. This changed as the Spanish began to gain a foothold south of the Douro during the 11th century, but no feudal system existed for raising or supporting large numbers of the expensive armoured cavalry. Therefore, the kings granted the newly won lands to any settler who would promise military service in return, and those settlers who could not afford a horse and armour were given them by the king. Newly liberated towns were also handed over to settlers, divided into

Late 13th-century knight (Magdeburg Cathedral) showing a plate-reinforced surcoat worn over the hauberk. It ends at the waist behind; the flaps at the front were not usually reinforced with plate but were perhaps padded. Note also the separate coif, common from the mid-13th century. The flap or lappet (repeated at the back) was fastened to the chest. In the last quarter of the century these lappets were extended to form a cape which reached almost to the points of the shoulders, and also covered the chin and mouth. A vertical slit at the rear, secured with laces, enabled the coif to be donned easily.

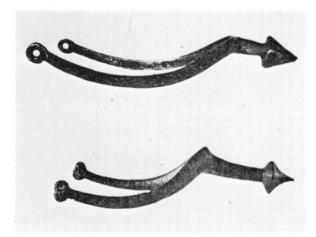

Two 13th century prick spurs, the upper one dating from the beginning of the century.

cavalry and infantry sectors, each of which had to give the appropriate military service. At first these grants reverted to the king on the death of the owner but the need for settlers was so great by the early 12th century that the grants were made hereditary.

The armoured cavalrymen thus raised were not knights, being of non-noble birth, and were termed *caballeros villanos*. Frontier warfare consisted mainly of raids and the *caballeros villanos* therefore adopted the Moorish style of hit-and-run fighting, riding on light horses and carrying light lances or javelins, which were thrown rather than used as shock weapons. Such light horse was ideal for the frontier warfare and formed the bulk of the Spanish cavalry arm, with a much smaller elite of the more heavily armoured nobles.

Another important source of fighting men was the city militia, most of whom were only required to defend their own walls in return for their grants. Although mainly an infantry force, any man wealthy enough to purchase a horse and armour was compelled to do so, and city militia therefore frequently included a proportion of *caballeros villanos*.

Municipal independence was also encouraged in Portugal from the mid 12th century, and from that date onwards Portugal could field armies which consisted of nobles and their feudal retainers together with steady bodies of infantry formed from free men and led by their own elected captains.

Mercenary bands were also employed to supplement the limited manpower as the land held by the

Christians was increased in volume. The most famous of these bands was that led by El Cid, who eventually had a following of around 7000 men. Most bands were considerably smaller, and frequently included a fair number of Moors.

Throughout our period the Christian armies of Iberia were hampered by the lack of manpower and the rivalry, frequently leading to civil war, between the various kingdoms. Many of the contingents would march away from a muster if their leader did not like the plan of campaign, and a Spanish king could count himself lucky if none of his troops actually sided with the enemy!

THE BYZANTINE ARMY

Byzantium had been 'crusading' against Islam since the 8th century and was particularly engaged in fighting the Seljuk Turks during the 12th century to keep open the land routes to the Holy Land for the western crusaders. Small groups of specialist troops and light cavalry also accompanied the armies of the 1st Crusade to the Holy Land, but it was not until 1137 that the Byzantine army advanced to Antioch, to force the Christian prince to pay homage to the emperor. In 1138 a combined Frankish-Byzantine army forced the amir of Shaizar to yield. The Byzantine army again advanced to Antioch in 1142 and 1158, the second expedition culminating in a combined campaign with the Franks against the Saracens in 1159. Byzantine forces also advanced to assist Tripoli against the Saracens in 1163 and 1164, and in 1168 the navy supported the Franks' invasion of Egypt. This was the last action of the crusades in which the Byzantines directly assisted the crusaders.

By the time of the 1st Crusade the quality of the Byzantine army had declined considerably and it was now mainly composed of mercenaries: Turks for the light cavalry; Franks and Normans for the heavy cavalry and therefore not used on the crusader front; Russians and Norsemen for the infantry; and Anglo-Saxons and Danes for the Varangian Guard. Nevertheless, the Byzantine army remained a formidable force, possibly the most highly organized army of the period, and it is worth looking at the basic military system which was to keep the Byzantine empire alive for another 400 years.

Each province or *theme* of the empire had its own militia or *thema*. Each *thema* consisted of two or three *turmae*, each *turma* of five to eight *numeri*, and each *numerus* of between 300 and 400 men: the strengths were deliberately variable so that the enemy should not immediately be able to guess a *thema*'s exact strength.

Each *thema* was responsible for the defence of its own *theme*, and could also be used to reinforce the standing army when necessary. The standing army consisted of regular forces of heavy and light cavalry, heavy and light infantry, and the Imperial Guard. Under Alexius Comnenus the total strength of the Byzantine army was about 70,000 men, with about 20,000 of that total in the standing army.

In the field the army was accompanied by a supply and siege train of carts and pack animals. An engineer corps and medical corps also marched with the field army.

The main forces engaged on the crusades frontier of the empire were the engineer corps, who assisted at several sieges during the 1st Crusade; the Varangian Guard, which accompanied the emperor to Antioch and took part in the subsequent campaigns, fought the crusaders when they attacked Constantinople in 1204, and was probably represented at the siege of Antioch in the 1st Crusade; and the Turkish light cavalry, some of whom took part in the 1st Crusade and the 12th-century campaigns mentioned above, and who also provided 'escorts' to see the crusaders through the lands of the empire, but frequently ended up fighting their unwelcome and unruly guests.

The Armies of Islam

In the centuries preceding the crusades, continual wars with Byzantium forged a highly organized and efficient Saracen army which to a large extent copied the Byzantine military system. By the end of the 10th century the Saracen Empire—and its army—was breaking up, to be replaced by independent provinces each with its own armed forces. The arrival of the Turks within the empire caused further changes and by the end of the 12th century most of the large armies which fought the crusaders

German broadsword c. 1150–1200, with 32⅜in double-edged blade, brazil nut pommel, and straight quillons of square section. The grip is missing. There is a shallow groove or fuller down the middle of both sides of the blade. This type of sword remained in use throughout our period, the brazil nut pommel until mid-13th century. (Reproduced by permission of the Trustees of the Wallace Collection)

A narrower, slightly longer 33¾in broadsword of c. 1340 with the bevelled wheel pommel which came into fashion c. 1175. A plain disc-shaped pommel was introduced earlier in the century and gradually became more popular, evolving into the wheel pommel, which became the dominant style during the 13th century. (Reproduced by permission of the Trustees of the Wallace Collection) were a mixture of mercenary and feudal troops, of Turks, Arabs and various aliens converted to Islam. However, much of the 10th-century army organization survived in the Egyptian army of the Fatimid dynasty (909–1170), while the united forces of Egypt and Syria under Saladin in the late 12th century also retained some of the earlier military system. The following summary of Abbasid army organization is therefore intended to illustrate the basic framework upon which later rulers imposed their own variations.

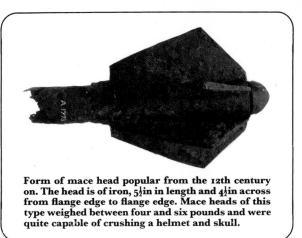

Form of mace head popular from the 12th century on. The head is of iron, 5½in in length and 4½in across from flange edge to flange edge. Mace heads of this type weighed between four and six pounds and were quite capable of crushing a helmet and skull.

THE ABBASID ARMIES

The Abbasid caliphate of Baghdad (750–1258), although influenced by the Byzantine military system, did not maintain a large standing army and the caliph's bodyguard was the only standing force in the true sense of the term. This bodyguard consisted of four types of troops: the Imperial bodyguard itself, supported by 'regiments' of heavy cavalry, heavy infantry and archers. The Imperial Guard of 4000 men consisted mainly of Turks from Transoxiana.

To this hard core was added, in times of war, mercenaries, volunteers led by their tribal chiefs, and feudal levies from the provinces. The volunteers, who served Islam and their caliph for religious reasons, were fed by the caliph but had to supply their own weapons and mounts. The mercenaries consisted mainly of aliens who had embraced Islam, frequently professional soldiers who accepted Islam only in order to enter the caliph's service. Thus an Abbasid army could include in its ranks not just Berbers and Africans, but also Russians, Franks, Greeks and Persians.

In the late 10th century the army was divided into four main corps: men of northern Arabia, men of southern Arabia, Persians, and Turks and Africans. Each corps had an attached body of mounted archers, either Persians or Turks. A corps usually consisted of 10,000 men, commanded by an amir. A 'regiment' of 1000 was commanded by a *Qā'id*, a company or squadron of 100 by a *Nakîb*, a sub-group of 50 men by a *Khalifah*, and a section of 10 men within that group by an *Aârif*.

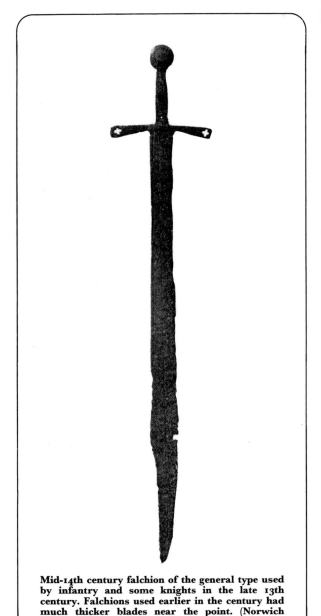

Mid-14th century falchion of the general type used by infantry and some knights in the late 13th century. Falchions used earlier in the century had much thicker blades near the point. (Norwich Museum)

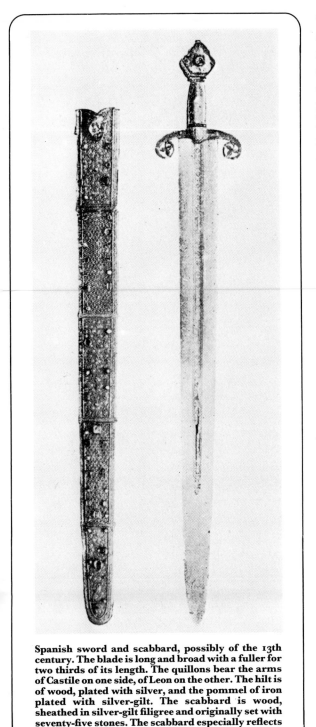

Spanish sword and scabbard, possibly of the 13th century. The blade is long and broad with a fuller for two thirds of its length. The quillons bear the arms of Castile on one side, of Leon on the other. The hilt is of wood, plated with silver, and the pommel of iron plated with silver-gilt. The scabbard is wood, sheathed in silver-gilt filigree and originally set with seventy-five stones. The scabbard especially reflects the Moorish influence on Spanish arms and armour.

throwing up a rampart at a camp site where the army was to stop for any length of time. The supply and siege trains mostly employed camels, which enabled the Arab armies to move faster than their enemies. If long distances were to be covered, the infantry might also be provided with camels and horses, and on short forced marches each cavalry-man took a foot soldier up behind him. Physicians and surgeons, with a hospital and ambulances (litters carried by camels) also accompanied the army in the field.

THE MOORISH ARMIES

The armies of the Ommayad dynasty (755–1031) were basically as described above: a bodyguard, volunteers and feudal levies, reinforced by mercenaries, in this case not Turks but Berbers from North Africa.

The army of the Berber Almoravide dynasty, which invaded Spain in 1086, also had its elite bodyguard, but had as well a regular force of infantry which was armed with long spears, except the front rank, which was armed with throwing javelins. The mounted forces of the Iberian amirs were usually employed on the flanks of this infantry

Axe head of the style used by Norman knights when fighting on foot, by some infantry, and by the Byzantine Varangian Guard. The head is 7$\frac{1}{10}$in in width, and 6$\frac{1}{10}$in from point to point across the blade. Weight would be about three pounds, and a three to four foot haft was normally used.

On the march the army was divided into five divisions: centre and two wings as for the battlefield, and van and rear guards. The vanguard always remained several miles ahead of the main body and had the task of digging a ditch and

Sculpture of the second half of the 13th century showing a knight clad from head to foot in mail, wrapped in a cloak, and armed with a mace.

line. During the next sixty years or so, until the Almohades came to power in 1145–7, the army also contained a great number of mercenaries, mostly Moslems but including some Spaniards who lived in Arab occupied territory. There were also many alliances between the various Moslem and Christian princes during this period, which meant that frequently Moslem armies took the field with Christian allies against other Moslems, and vice versa.

The army of the Almohades dynasty (1146–1275) consisted mainly of infantry, because these Berbers originated from a mountainous region. This infantry was formed in a great phalanx, the front ranks armed with crossbows, those behind with long spears. The phalanx was supported by horsemen (probably mercenaries) on each flank.

THE SELJUK ARMIES

The Turks who served in the Abbasid armies were soldiers of fortune who penetrated the whole of the Moslem world in much the same way that Norman adventurers penetrated western Europe at this time. By about 1050 Turkish regiments were maintained by most of the newly independent provinces of the caliphate. The most notable of these warriors were the Seljuk Turks, who by 1055 had seized power in Persia and Baghdad and subsequently took Syria and Mesopotamia from the Fatimid caliphate of Egypt.

The Seljuks did not change the basic military organization of the Arabs, but they did improve on the system whereby each province had to finance its own contingent of the army from its revenue, by introducing a more feudal system under which the government and revenue of a province or district were placed in the hands of an amir, who was required in exchange to pay a yearly tribute to the sultan and in time of war to bring to the sultan's army a fixed number of troops. Some amirs sub-let portions of their districts or individual towns to lesser amirs, who in turn had to furnish troops to their overlord. However, these sub-tenants owed no allegiance direct to the sultan, and were bound only to their local amir.

Seljuk armies, therefore, consisted of a large regular force in the form of the sultan's bodyguard and household troops, together with the feudal contingents of the amirs, each of whom also had a smaller regular force as his own bodyguard. These bodyguards, or regular forces, were known as *askars*, the men being *askaris*. The sultan's bodyguard was mainly Turkish, divided into regiments, and all mounted, as indeed were all the *askars*. In time of war all *askars* were usually strengthened by mercenaries, mostly Turcoman mounted archers and regiments of Daylamites, natives of the mountainous regions south-west of the Caspian Sea.

The numerical strength of an *askar* varied according to the stature of the amir and little is known of actual numbers. However, during the 1st Crusade we know the *askars* of Aleppo and Damascus were each about 2000 men, and they were the leading amirates of Syria. The great city of Mosul, in northern Mesopotamia, could field an army of 15,000 men at the beginning of the 12th century, and in mid-13th century the caliph of

An illustration from the early 13th-century Maciejowski Bible, showing a variety of weapons in use: broadsword, mace, axe and bow. At this date the bow was about five feet long with a pull of between 30–50lbs; the string was drawn back only as far as the chest. Arrows were about 28in long. (The Pierpont Morgan Library, New York)

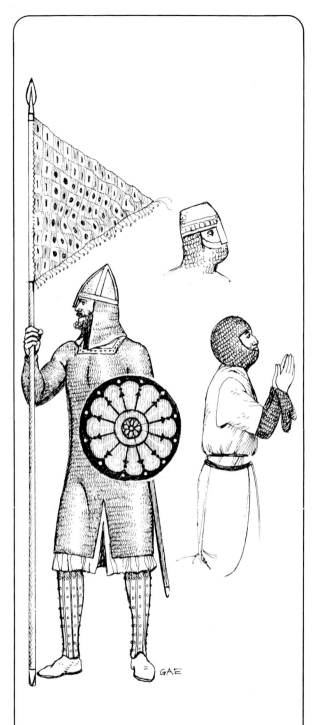

Spanish knight of the early 12th century with a shield and banner based on illustrations in a manuscript of *c*. 1109 from the monastery of Selos near Burgos. The other figures are also Spanish, the upper one from an 11th century reliquary, the lower from a miniature of 1280.

Baghdad could command 120,000 horsemen, presumably including a large percentage of mercenaries.

The feudal levies were only called out in times of emergency and most fighting was done by the *askars* and mercenaries. Another force was the territorial reserve, troops who were maintained by grants of land. They were also called out only in emergencies. Both the feudal levies and the territorial reservists were mounted but were armed with spear and sword, not the bow. They normally provided their own weapons and horses, but were sometimes equipped from the arsenals, wherein were stored the arms for the *askars*.

The infantry was formed from townsmen and countrymen pressed into service, volunteers seeking religious reward, and camp followers, etc. Their role was usually limited to garrison, camp and siege duties, though some bodies of infantry—notably the citizen bands of Aleppo, Damascus and Hama—appear to have achieved a high state of discipline and were well equipped.

The proportion of the different types of troops within an army varied from campaign to campaign. At the battle of Baban on 18 April 1167 the Seljuks fielded 9000 *askaris*, 3000 archers and 10,000 Arabs armed with spears. When Shirkuh, the commander of the Ayyubid army, entered Cairo in 1169 he had with him an *askar* of 2000 men and 6000 mercenaries led by their own chiefs.

In the field the army was accompanied by a large supply and siege train, and by physicians and surgeons with hospital equipment.

THE FATIMID ARMIES

Because of its great wealth, unity and organization, the Fatimid caliphate of Egypt was able to field enormous armies. However, the Egyptians were not a martial nation and therefore the armies were for the most part formed from an assortment of nationalities, mercenaries hired with Egypt's wealth. The elite of the army, as always, was the caliph's bodyguard, composed of white slaves from various Turkish tribes, who provided the mounted regiments, and the more unusual Sudanese guard of foot soldiers, for, unlike other Islamic powers of the Middle East, Egyptian armies contained a good proportion of well trained and well equipped professional infantry. The total strength of the bodyguard was normally about 5000 men, but there was also a 'Young Guard' (known as the youths or squires of the Chamber) of about 500 youths from leading families, who were trained for military posts and had pledged to execute at once any command given them. Those who distinguished themselves (and survived) rose to the rank of amir. As in the Seljuk armies, each amir of note also maintained his own smaller bodyguard, which accompanied him in the field when he served the caliph.

The remainder of the army was recruited mainly from the Arabs, Berbers and Sudanese, but their military quality was generally inferior to that of the Seljuk and Frankish armies. The Sudanese fought on foot and provided the archer arm of the army; the Arabs and Berbers fought on horseback with lance and sword but relied on mobility and superior numbers for victory over the more heavily armed Frankish knights. There were no mounted archers in the army, but from time to time, as politics dictated, contingents of allied Turks did sometimes join the army on campaign.

The Bedouin were also employed by the Fatimids, filling the light-cavalry role. Bedouin society was patriarchal and the warriors were never ordered to do anything—they followed the example of the sheik voluntarily. This was not conducive to success in regular battle, and in general the Bedouin were unreliable on the battlefield, liable to join the winning side at the last minute in order to participate in the pillaging; nonetheless, they were employed extensively by all the Moslem dynasties, as well as by the crusaders, in a reconnaissance role, and by the Moslems as light cavalry on the extreme flanks of armies in the field.

The army was supported by a system of territorial reservists similar to that of the Seljuks.

The amirs who provided the officers for the army were of three classes: amirs of the gold chain, who commanded the various divisions; sword bearers, who escorted the caliph; and the lesser amirs who formed the chivalry of the army with the squires of the Chamber. The lighter armed Arab and Berber cavalry formed a second line to the amirs and squires.

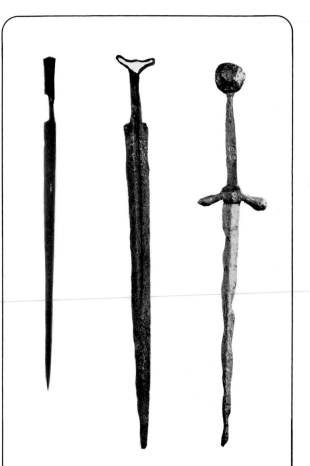

Left: a baselard-type knife, 27in overall and with a single edged blade. *Centre*: a double edged dagger with 31in blade. These weapons were little more than short swords, and as such formed a secondary weapon for the crossbowmen and spearmen.

Right: a double-edged quillon dagger, 13.1in overall, with a diamond section blade. This was the type carried by mounted men, usually at their right side, but was only used as a last resort.

THE AYYUBID ARMIES

When Saladin came to power in 1169 his first action was to crush a revolt of the Sudanese guards and to form an entirely new bodyguard, loyal to him, from about a thousand Kurdish free men from his own family's retainers and from the 2000-strong *askar* of Shirkuh, which was serving under him in Egypt and which transferred its loyalty to him en masse. Saladin then began to rebuild the rest of the forces of Egypt into an efficient fighting machine capable of invading the Frankish states and reinstating Islam.

Saladin found the old feudal system totally inadequate and he lacked the resources to maintain a huge mercenary army. He therefore introduced the Seljuk system of appointing amirs to governorships of provinces, districts and individual cities in return for an annual tribute and military service in the field with a fixed quota of troops.

It naturally took some years for this system to become fully established, and his early campaigns to crush the major Moslem princes and reunite Islam were achieved mainly with an elite force of *askaris* and mounted archers—at its peak a force of about 8000 men—backed up by the old feudal levies. The last of the independent princes, the amir of Aleppo, was not crushed until 1183, but thereafter Saladin could count on the active support of the strongest Moslem princes in his holy war against the Franks.

In his campaigns against the crusaders Saladin's armies resembled those of the Seljuks, although swollen to greater size by a large number of contingents from the amirs. Firstly there were Saladin's own Kurdish guards, the mamluks or white slaves which formed the rest of his bodyguard, and the bodyguards of his amirs; secondly there were hired mercenaries, the Turcoman mounted archers; and thirdly there were the feudal levies of the amirs.

At Ascalon in 1177, when he was still relying heavily on the old Fatimid system, Saladin had an army of some 26,000 men, of whom only 8000 were *askaris* or mercenaries, the other 18,000 being spearmen, Sudanese archers, and Arab and Berber cavalrymen. However, by the time of Hattin in 1187 he was able to muster some 12,000 *askaris* and mercenaries, backed by between 6000 and 12,000 feudal levies.

Mention has been made of mamluks. These were white (which meant Turkish rather than Berber, Arab or Sudanese) slaves, either captured in war or purchased in the market, who were converted to Islam and (if purchased) trained from boyhood in the art of war for the sole purpose of forming elite and loyal bodyguards for the amirs. Such bodies of troops had been maintained from the time of the Saracen Empire, but these were not strictly speaking mamluks, who were of exclusively Turkish origin. (The 'Turkish' bodyguards of the Abbasids, for example, were Turkish speaking but were not ethnically Turkish, including in their ranks Slavs,

Armenians, Russians and Greeks.) The change to purely Turkish bodyguards did not begin until the 1230s, when the bodyguards became almost exclusively Turkish owing to an influx of Kuman warriors from the Kipchak steppe, fleeing before the Mongol invasions.

These bodyguards had become very strong under the Abbasids (as we have seen, the caliph at Baghdad was merely their puppet) and under Saladin they became both more numerous and powerful, often constituting half the field army. The system was perfected by Saladin's successors, who had seen the advantages of such an army over a mainly feudal one, and they used their strengthened *askars* in the civil wars which followed Saladin's death. This served to increase the power of the bodyguards still further, until it was the *askars*, the mamluks, who named the heir to the throne.

Aiyub (1240–49) was the last effective ruler of the Ayyubid dynasty founded by Saladin and it was Aiyub who imported great numbers of new mamluks, from whom he then selected approximately a thousand of the most loyal and fierce warriors to form a new personal bodyguard. This bodyguard became known as the Bahri Regiment and was stationed in a castle he had built on the island al-Rawda opposite Fustat.

By 1249, when Aiyub died, some of the amirs of the Bahri Regiment had their own bodies of mamluks, but the regiment at first remained loyal to Aiyub's successor and distinguished itself at Mansourah in February 1250, where the Egyptian commander-in-chief was killed and the leader of the Bahris took his place.

Aiyub's heir arrived from Mosul in the same month but soon lost the support of the Bahris and other Egyptian mamluks by giving all appointments to his own personal bodyguard of mamluks, and on 2 May he was murdered by the Bahris. Aiyub's sultana was married to the senior Bahri amir, Aibek, and so began the rule of the mamluk sultans.

THE MAMLUK ARMIES

For 130 years after Aibek came to the throne, the amirs of the Bahri Regiment and their successors were the sultans, for the throne was not hereditary

1 **Crusader 1st-3rd Crusades**
2 **Knight 3rd Crusade**
3, 4 **Crusaders 1st-3rd Crusades**
5, 6, 7 **Crusaders mid-12th century**

G. A. EMBLETON

A

1 **Crossbowman** *c.*1180-1300
2 **Sergeant** *c.*1220-1300
3, 4 **Foot soldiers** *c.*1200-1300
5 **Slinger** 1100-1300

B

G. A. EMBLETON

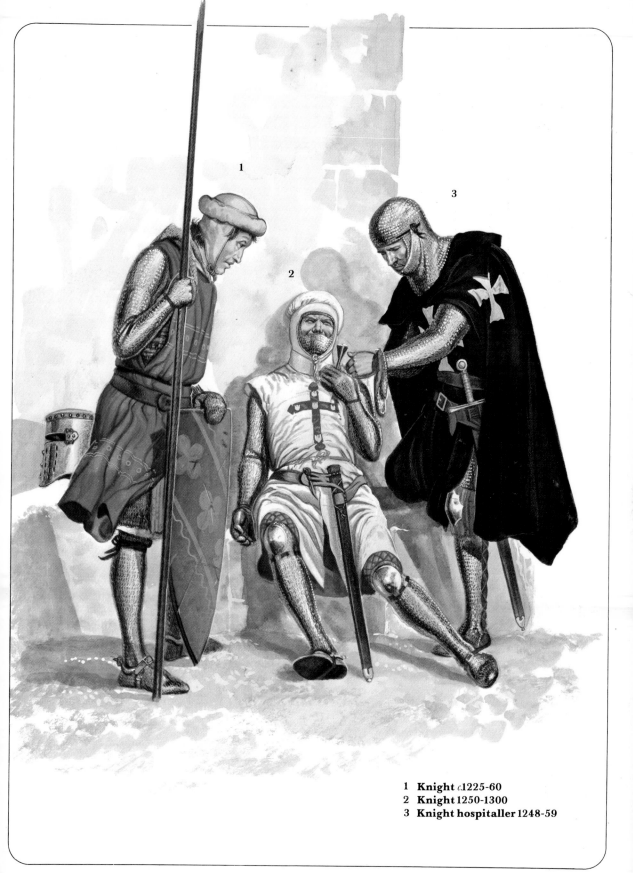

1 **Knight** c.1225-60
2 **Knight** 1250-1300
3 **Knight hospitaller** 1248-59

G. A. EMBLETON

C

1 **Teutonic knight** *c.*1230-83
2 **Hochmeister, Teutonic Order** *c.*1219
3 **Schwertbrüder** *c.*1270

D

G. A. EMBLETON

1 Spanish nobleman early 13th century
2 Spanish knight mid-13th century
3 Moorish foot soldier 12th century
4 Moorish horseman late 12th century

G. A. EMBLETON

E

1 Byzantine peltast early 12th century
2 Varangian guardsman late 11th century
3 Byzantine cavalryman late 11th century

G. A. EMBLETON

1 Seljuk mounted archer 12th century
2 Mamluk askari mid-13th century
3 Mamluk amir second half 13th century

1 **Mamluk askari second half 13th century**
2 **Syrian amir 12th-13th centuries**
3 **Mamluk askari 13th century**
4 **Turkish archer 12th-13th centuries**
5 **Turcoman auxiliary 12th-13th centuries**

out went to the strongest and most powerful amir. Therefore, every Mamluk sultan was posed with the dilemma of whom to appoint as commander of a distant region; a strong commander might overthrow the sultan, a weak one lose the province. It was normal therefore to appoint two commanders, one as governor of the district, the other to command the citadel of the district's city—and to change both frequently.

The safety and power of the sultan also depended on the loyalty of his mamluks and the greater part of the land of Egypt therefore came to be held by the amirs of the sultan's bodyguard in fiefs granted by the sultan. The amirs in their turn were obliged to divide up to two thirds of their fiefs between their own mamluks to secure their loyalty.

The nucleus of any Mamluk army therefore consisted of three main parts: the royal bodyguard (the sultan's favourite and most loyal regiment, and indeed often the one which had placed him on the throne); the other mamluk regiments of the sultan; and the private companies and regiments of the officers within his bodyguard. Bedouin, Turcoman and Kurdish mercenaries were hired to augment this force.

The strength of the royal bodyguard at the beginning of the 14th century was 2000 men and 40 officers, though it may have been slightly smaller during the second half of the 13th century. The sultan could field a total of about 12,000 mamluks in 1290, and an estimated 20,000 in 1299. Theoretically there was an Amir of a Thousand for every 1000 mamluks and under him lesser amirs for every unit of 40 men, with a sub-section of 10 men within that.

The rapid increase in the number of mamluks towards the end of the century was mainly caused by the sultan Kala'un (1279–90) taking the Burdiyya Regiment as his royal bodyguard after they had murdered his predecessor. This regiment consisted of 3700 men, stationed in the towers of the citadel of Cairo. They were mainly Circassians, with possibly some Armenians, and constituted a powerful and loyal force. The bulk of the other two thirds of the bodyguard remained Kipchakis, though many Mongols were taken into the mamluks after being defeated in 1260 and 1281. The Burdiyya seized the throne at the end of the century.

Third-rate troops, such as the Bedouin, and members of the now rapidly declining Bahri Regiment, were used to garrison the fortresses of the Egyptian coast against the crusaders' sea-borne invasions. In times of great danger the royal mamluks were forced to join these garrisons, but they stayed for only short periods and frequently returned to Cairo—the seat of all power—before being ordered to do so.

On campaign the army was accompanied by a large camel caravan; mules were rarely used and wheeled vehicles were used only for siege engines. The largest armies needed between 800–1000 camels just to carry the light armament and usually every mamluk was entitled to two camels for his gear, non-mamluk soldiers having three camels for every two men. Physicians, surgeons and hospital equipment travelled with the army.

The Mamluks also placed great value on bands and at one time the sultan's band had 44 drums, 4 *hautbois* (oboes) and 20 trumpets. Permission to have a band was a highly coveted distinction and those amirs who received it were known as Lords of the Drums. There were about 30 such amirs, each in command of 40 horsemen, with a band of 10 drums, 2 hautbois and 4 trumpets. The mamluks made great use of these bands in war, and the drums are believed to have been particularly effective at creating chaos in the ranks of armies whose horses were unaccustomed to the noise.

The sultan Baibars (1260–77) established a well organized system of posting houses connecting every part of the empire with the capital, and relays of horses were maintained in these houses. Reports from each part of the empire were received and answered twice a week. There was also a pigeon post (copied from the Arab caliphs) with cots in the citadel at Cairo and at various stages, the pigeons being trained to fly only between these stages.

The Plates

Additional costume research was carried out by G. A. Embleton, who wishes to thank Richard and Sevil Peach and Baha Tannmann for their assistance.

The study of arms, armour and costume in the 12th and 13th centuries has perforce to be based mainly on information contained in illuminated manuscripts, contemporaneous sculpture, decoration of artifacts, etc., as very little of the original material has survived. Therefore almost all writing on these subjects is interpretation of such evidence and open to argument. In this book the generally accepted verdicts are given, with one or two questions raised.

In the case of the Turkish and Saracenic arms, armour and costume there is even less information available, for Islamic art of the period was highly stylized. The position is further confused by the clash of influences in the Middle East at the time; Byzantine military styles survived until quite late in Egypt, while Syria was influenced by Persia and then by the Turks, and in Iberia the Moorish fashions were strongly influenced by the West and each influx of newcomers from North Africa. What little pictorial evidence there is hints at a rich and varied costume about which we may never know very much.

An Egyptian hauberk (*zardiyyat*) of the late 15th century which, apart from the collar, is of the general style worn by Egyptians and Syrians from 1100 to 1300.

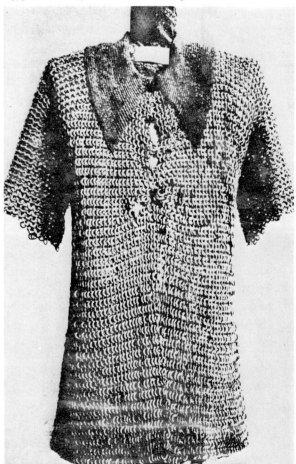

The figures portrayed in Plates G and H are reconstructions based on contemporary material often very simple, yet difficult to interpret: the artist has done his best with the limited information available.

A3, A4 Crusaders, 1st–3rd Crusades
Many of the fighting men who went on the 1st Crusades were dressed and armed in the style so vividly illustrated in the Bayeux Tapestry (completed between 1070 and 1080). In this Plate figures A3 and A4 especially show this style: conical helmet, often with nasal bar to protect the face; knee-length mail hauberk with wide elbow-length sleeves and slit at front and rear from hem to crutch; a mail coif which was usually made as part of the hauberk; large kite-shaped shield; a spear which could be used from horseback either under or over arm, or could even be thrown; a sword or axe. This style of equipment was still being worn by foot soldiers and poorer knights as late as the 3rd Crusade.

A1 Crusader, 1st–3rd Crusade
This 1st Crusade warrior is of a higher rank and more protected by mail than A3 and A4 (knighthood was not synonymous with nobility until after the 1st Crusade). Hauberks with fairly tight-fitting sleeves extending to the wrist were in use at the time of the 1st Crusade but did not become popular until the 3rd Crusade, and never fully superseded the short-sleeved version. The mail hose, worn over cloth hose, were fastened to a belt worn under the hauberk and gartered below the knee, so as to decrease drag. Note the separate coif of leather for greater comfort; the lacing at the neck of the hauberk; and the straps on the back of the shield.

A2 Knight, 3rd Crusade
By this date the sleeves of the hauberk had been extended to form mittens with a palm of leather or cloth, slit so that the hand could be withdrawn, and laced round the wrist to reduce drag. This hauberk incorporates a coif, which was usually secured to the head by a thong threaded through the mail at the brow, as here, and has a flap of mail, known as the *aventail*, which is drawn across the lower part of the face and secured to the brow band. Aventail

An assortment of drawings based on Saracen and Turkish contemporary manuscripts and sculptures. Top left is a different type of 12th-century Saracen helmet; below are Turks wearing lamellar armour, also 12th century; and on the right a group of Seljuks.

were introduced at the end of the 11th century.

The strips of mail covering the fronts of the legs and tops of the feet were introduced in 1100 and were secured to the belt. Both forms of leg defence shown in this Plate were in common use by knights by 1150. Round-topped helmets were introduced about the same date, although they did not replace the earlier conical type, which continued to be used until the mid-13th century.

A5, A6, A7 *Crusaders, mid-12th century*
Many of the knights of the 1st Crusade wore a long linen coat under their hauberks (A2). The purpose of this coat can now only be guessed at. By mid-12th century some knights had adopted the surcoat, an early example of which is shown by A6, which is

based on the figure of Waleran de Bellemonte on his seal, attached to a charter earlier than 1150. The theory that such coats were copied from the Saracens, who wore long loose-fitting gowns over their armour, cannot be discounted, but they are unlikely to have been used to shade the armour from the sun. It is more likely that they followed the Saracen purpose more closely (see text on Plates G and H) and were worn merely so that the wearer might look better, a sort of dress uniform, and it should be noted that this figure is wearing a 'surcoat' and hat which both follow civilian fashion of the time.

The 'pot' helmets worn by A5 and A7 first came into use about the middle of the 12th century, and were common by 1180. The shield held by A7 has

Turkish *zardiyyat* with plate reinforcement, secured by brass hooks. This example dates from the 14th century but is of the style worn in the 13th century by Mamluks and Syrian amirs. (Türkiye Askeri Müzesi)

by this date lost its curved top, presumably to give better vision.

B1 Crossbowman c.1180–1300

The crossbow was used extensively in the 1st Crusade, and during the 12th century the weapon's popularity and importance grew as the value of infantry in the Holy Land came to be fully appreciated. The weapon was a particular favourite of the mercenaries, and the best crossbowmen of the crusades were in the mercenary bands hired from Genoa and the Low Countries.

Originally the plain wooden bow stave enabled the crossbow to be spanned (loaded) by hand but by the end of the 12th century a stronger composite stave was being used and the weapon had to be spanned with the aid of a hook on the crossbowman's belt. This was looped over the bow string, one foot placed in a metal stirrup at the front of the crossbow's stock, and the bow spanned either by pushing the leg out straight or by pressing the stirrup to the ground and leaning back.

B2 Sergeant c. 1220–1300

In the Holy Land sergeants were usually armoured soldiers, inferior in equipment and rank to knights, who rode in the second line of cavalry and often formed the bulk of the mounted force. They were only called upon to serve in the field army in times of emergency and normally their duties were limited to serving in their city's garrison, manning the citadel, or guarding their lord's residence. It is not now possible to tell whether all sergeants were mounted, or all foot soldiers, or some of each, but certainly in the duties listed above, and at sieges, their duties were mainly dismounted ones.

Detail of the plates on the 14th century Turkish *zardiyyat*. (Türkiye Askeri Müzesi)

The sergeant illustrated is wearing the long-sleeved hauberk with mittens and coif of the late 12th century, and a simple helmet known as a *cervellière*, first introduced *c.* 1200. The *cervellière* was a most popular form of helmet with all ranks from about 1220 onwards, and from mid-century many knights wore it under their coif—sometimes with no other form of head defence. The sergeant is also wearing *cuisses*, quilted leg-defences which were introduced *c.* 1220. They were secured to a belt under the hauberk. He is armed with the great two-handed axe adopted from the Anglo-Saxons by the Normans after 1066; in the 12th century many Norman knights favoured this weapon when fighting on foot.

B3, B4 *Foot soldiers* c. 1200–1300

Unlike the professional infantry, such as the mercenary crossbowmen and spearmen, most foot soldiers could not afford mail armour and were equipped instead with fabric body armours. These were used throughout the 12th and 13th centuries, although the earliest known references date from the second half of the 12th century, by which date the armours were in general use.

Broadly speaking there were two types of fabric body armour, the *aketon* and the *gambeson*, although no hard line can now be drawn between the various types, which are known collectively as *pourpoint*. The *aketon*, illustrated on B1, B3 and B4, was of buckram, stuffed with cotton and quilted vertically. Some had tight-fitting full-length sleeves, occasionally ending in mittens: others had wide sleeves ending at the elbow. Most had a high collar, sometimes reinforced with some kind of solid lining.

The *gambeson* consisted of two layers of coarse linen stuffed with flax or rags and quilted either in squares or diamonds. It reached only to the groin and was either sleeveless or had wide, short sleeves. Again there was a wide collar, probably lined with some form of plate. The *gambeson* was used by some infantry but was worn mainly by sergeants and poor knights.

The soldier illustrated by B3 wears a *chapel-de-fer* or kettle hat, introduced at the end of the 12th century and popular throughout the 13th century with all ranks.

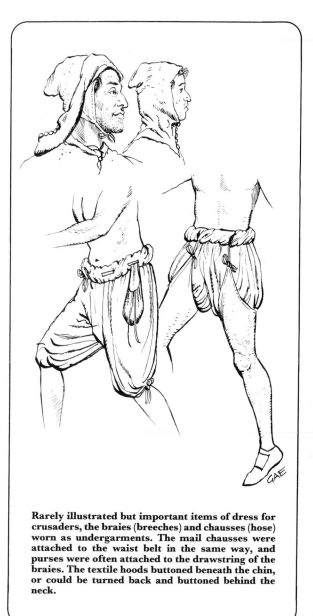

Rarely illustrated but important items of dress for crusaders, the braies (breeches) and chausses (hose) worn as undergarments. The mail chausses were attached to the waist belt in the same way, and purses were often attached to the drawstring of the braies. The textile hoods buttoned beneath the chin, or could be turned back and buttoned behind the neck.

B5 *Slinger* 1100–1300

Although rarely mentioned, the humble slinger was a valuable missile man in medieval armies, capable of discharging a hail of bullets or stones with considerable accuracy and in rapid volleys. A four-foot staff sling was sometimes used to hurl larger projectiles.

A high degree of skill was needed with the sling, and such men had usually been accustomed to their weapon since childhood (peasants who needed to protect their livestock against wild animals but could not afford any other type of weapon). Pilgrims and camp followers would have yielded

such men, wearing their everyday clothes. The man illustrated also has a small targe and a sword, though his real role remained purely to supply missile fire before a battle or at sieges.

C1 *Knight* c.1225–60

Major changes began to take place in the 13th century as the knight sought better protection. Mail was a good defence generally speaking, but it could not always stop a lance thrust, nor a good swing with an axe or sword. Wearing a *gambeson* beneath the hauberk was a common extra defence of the 12th century (part of it can be seen where the hauberk is slit at the front on this figure) but by about 1225 the richer knights were beginning to wear an additional defence over the hauberk. The straps of this defence, which was known as a *cuirie*, can just be seen by the arm of the knight.

The *cuirie* was probably of *cuir bouilli*—leather boiled in wax and then shaped—and may sometimes have been reinforced by metal plates. Evidence of the *cuirie*'s form is scanty, as surcoats conceal most of it, but it was probably quite short, sleeveless, and comprised a front and back 'plate' with flaps extending round the sides, where they were strapped together.

By about 1225, too, the kite-shaped shield often had a flat upper edge and was less concave; by mid-century it was beginning to assume the shorter form now known as the 'heater' shield, from its resemblance to a flat iron.

The knight also wears prick spurs, which remained the only form of spur during the 12th and 13th centuries; and under his mail coif he wears an arming cap, which was simply the civilian cap of the period with a roll of padding round the brow, and served to protect the head and hold in position the helmet illustrated. Some pot helms had had face guards added from 1180 onwards, and such guards were in general use by about 1210. By 1220 the head was completely encased in the type of helmet illustrated, known as the 'great helm' or *heaume*. These helmets were padded inside but do not appear to have been secured under the chin, and that roll on the arming cap (first introduced about 1200) may have played a vital role in keeping the helmet in place.

Part of the painted windows of St Denys, near Paris, now lost but preserved in the 18th-century illustrations by Montfaucon. The windows were painted in the 12th century and the two reproductions show scenes from the 1st Crusade. On the right of each picture are Seljuks, which the medieval artist has shown as closely resembling Europeans, a common practice of the period and presumably due to lack of accurate information. However, an attempt has been made on one figure in each picture to portray the lamellar armour worn by the Seljuks in the crusading era.

C2 Knight c.1250–1300

By the mid-12th century surcoats were commonly worn over the hauberk, but were still not worn by all knights. Between 1170 and 1200 they became more common and by about 1200 were in general use as a long, loose-fitting gown of knee or mid-calf length, with large arm holes as shown by C1. They were still split at front and rear from hem to crutch. The emblem on the surcoat of this figure is taken from a Spanish manuscript. Note that here the arming cap is worn over the mail coif.

Two developments in armour during this period were the division of the mail mittens into separate fingers c.1250, although the mitten form remained the most popular, and the introduction of the first plate-defence—for the knee. Known as *poleyns*, the plate knee-defences first appeared c.1230 and were in general use by mid-century. These early *poleyns* were quite small, as illustrated, and are shown here attached to the mail. The ends of the knight's quilted *cuisses* are also visible.

C3 Knight Hospitaller 1248–59

The Hospitaller is wearing his Order's black mantle over a black surcoat; the mantle alone was worn until 1248, when the black surcoat was introduced. In 1259 the Order changed to a red surcoat with a white cross. Note the fastening of the *aventail* to the brow band and the combination of *cuisse* and *poleyn* in an attempt to overcome the difficulties of securing extra defences over mail comfortably.

D1 Teutonic Knight c.1230–83

Unlike almost all other medieval campaigns, those of the Teutonic Knights against the Prussians were conducted in mid-winter, for only then could they negotiate the terrain relatively easily, with the

Arab horsemen, painted c. 1210 (Baghdad School), showing the flowing robe with *tiraz* (embroidered bands on the sleeves) worn over armour by the Saracen amirs.

A reasonable portrayal of Saracen horsemen, from Marinus Sanutus' *Handbook for Crusaders*, **c. 1321. (Bodleian Library).**

numerous swamps and rivers frozen solid. Their white surcoats and mantles must have acted as camouflage in such a setting, though this was accidental, the white cloak and surcoat having been adopted in 1191 in the Holy Land.

The knight illustrated is wearing a pot helmet beneath his coif and wears the white surcoat with the black Latin cross of the Teutonic Order. However, from the form of the surcoat it is obvious that plates, of *cuir bouilli*, metal or horn, have been incorporated in the material to provide an extra body defence.

D2 *Hochmeister of the Teutonic Order* c.1219

The Hochmeister wears on his surcoat and mantle a silver-edged cross of the Order. In 1219 the King of Jerusalem granted the Hochmeister the right to bear the gold cross of Jerusalem under the Order's black cross, thus creating a gold edge; this figure is, therefore, 1219 or earlier.

The great helm is of approximately the same date. Note the lacing of the surcoat under the right arm, and gold chain which is fastened to the rear of the helmet at one end, and the waist cord at the other. The Hochmeister holds a lance bearing the banner of the Teutonic Order.

D3 *Schwertbrüder* c. 1270

This member of the Brethren of the Sword is wearing the more conical form of great helm which began to be worn from about 1270. Note the fitting for a crest. The heater shield he bears was the predominant style of shield by this date. Surcoats with elbow-length sleeves were common in the

32

second half of the century and some had full-length sleeves. The *poleyns* of this period completely covered the knee at front and sides.

Note a *gambeson* is still worn under the hauberk, and the surcoat appears to have been padded to some extent. The banner could also have two crossed swords below the German cross.

E1 Spanish nobleman, early 13th century
This figure is based on the effigy on the tomb of Ferdinando de la Cerda at the monastery of Las Huelgas, near Burgos, and dated about 1200–11. Note the side lacing of the 'shirt' and the sword worn on a baldric in Moorish fashion. An illustration in a contemporary Spanish manuscript shows a group of foot soldiers of King Jaime I (1213–76) apparently wearing the same wide-legged breeches, and others wearing padded body armours and caps (see infantry figures in the background of this Plate). Knights were more likely to wear mail over such garments, though some poor knights and sergeants, who could not afford mail, did wear only fabric body armours. The breeches bear a marked resemblance to those shown in the Bayeux Tapestry, woven some 130 years earlier, which poses the question: Did many of the padded undergarments worn by knights, and normally hidden by hauberk and surcoat, take this form, which is after all so much more sensible for a mounted fighting man than a garment with a skirt?

E2 Spanish Knight, mid-13th century
Based on a figure in a Catalan fresco, showing the camp of Jaime I of Aragon (the tent in the background is from the same source), this illustration shows a typical Spanish knight of the mid-13th century. The bearing of heraldic arms on helmet as well as shield and on the sleeves of the surcoat as well as on the lance pennon, is typically Spanish, as can be seen from the late 13th-century manuscript *Cantigas of Alfonso X*, King of Leon and Castile, 1252–84.

The round helmet shown, with or without a nasal, was far more popular in Spain than the conical type shown in Plate A. The heater type of shield was unknown in Spain, but in the 13th century the kite-shaped shield shrank to the form illustrated, though usually with a more rounded bottom edge. The elbow-length sleeves of the

surcoat date the figure to around mid-century, otherwise he represents the appearance of Spanish knights for most of the 13th century.

E3 Moorish foot soldier, 12th century
The infantry of the Berber dynasties which invaded Spain in 1086, 1146 and 1275 mostly wore simple fabric body armours and turbans, or went bare headed. The large round shield illustrated was the most common form of shield, not only for Moorish infantry, but also throughout the world of Islam. It was made of wood, either solid or laminated, and might be polished, or faced with leather, the latter being varnished or painted. The kite-shaped shield was also used by the Berbers from the 12th century. The baldric was used for sword suspension throughout the 12th and 13th centuries, and supports here

Saracen *tabar* or axe. The example illustrated is a ceremonial axe, such as might have been carried in front of the sultan by special guards, but takes the traditional form of the Islamic fighting axe.

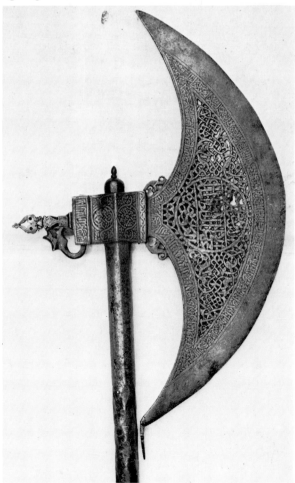

The famous Krak des Chevaliers, manned by the Knights Hospitaller from 1142 until its capture in 1272. Because of their relatively small numbers, the Franks were dependent on such fortifications to maintain control of their lands. Such castles were built for economic and administrative purposes just as much as for military ones, and the Krak controlled the lands of the Assassins, who paid tribute to the Hospitallers. The garrison and staff at such a centre of power could be as large as 2000—the population of a major town in Europe.

a type of sword which was prevalent in all Islamic armies.

E4 Moorish horseman, late 12th century

The heart-shaped shield (*adarga*) of the Moorish cavalry first appears in Spain during the late 12th-century invasion by the Berbers. It was made of several layers of hardened leather sewn together. The style was copied by the Spaniards, just as the Moors' styles were influenced by those of the West; for example, Moorish cavalry also used the flat-topped version of the kite-shaped shield in the second half of the 13th century. Light cavalrymen, such as the one illustrated, did not normally wear helmets, but wore a variety of soft head-gear. Heavy cavalry generally wore helmets and mail hauberks and the latter were not reinforced by plate armour as in the Holy Land (see Plates G and H).

F1 Byzantine peltast early 12th century

The Byzantine infantryman known as a 'peltast' first appeared in the 10th century and is recorded in the early 12th century by Anna Comnena, daughter of the emperor. He was probably an economy measure, being better armed than the light infantry of the older empire, but not so heavily armoured as the old heavy infantry.

A corselet of lamellar armour may have been worn in earlier times, but lack of funds in the 11th and 12th centuries would probably have resulted in the men wearing the thickly quilted and studded armour illustrated. (Lamellar armour consisted of small rectangular plates of iron or rawhide laced together with leather thongs in horizontal rows, the rows then being laced together vertically, overlapping each other upwards.) The kite-shaped shield may have been Byzantine in origin.

F2 Varangian guardsman late 11th century

This figure is based on a mosaic at the Church of Nea Moni on the island of Khios. By the time of the crusades the Varangian Guard was the most important and most loyal part of the standing army. It consisted almost entirely of Anglo-Saxons who had fled from England after their rebellions had been crushed by the Danes and William the Conqueror. These men retained the great two-handed axe as their favourite weapon in the field, and there are many references in contemporary sources to the axemen of the Guard. The shield would have been slung over the back by a strap when the axe was being used. The Guard rode to battle, but fought on foot.

The 'arrow heads' on the trousers may be brass or gilt studs in padded leg defences.

F3 Byzantine cavalryman late 11th century
In the Byzantine army each unit within a *turma* was identified by the use of a distinctive colour for tunic, cloak, shield and helmet plume, or, as in this case, a fabric covering for a helmet which shows a distinct eastern influence.

The swallow-tailed pennon carried on the man's lance is as illustrated in the Scylitzes manuscript of c 1200 but was probably copied from an 11th century original and may be that of a *turma*, each unit within the *turma* possibly using different coloured tails.

G1 Seljuk mounted archer 12th century
The long coat, long plaits, necklace and earrings are all typical of the Seljuk Turks, as is the belt decorated with metal plates. Like many 'barbaric' nomad tribes, the Seljuks loved to display their wealth on their person, and to the Turk of the Middle Ages beautiful clothing had great value and prestige: there were eight different terms for silk in the Seljuk language, and rich clothing was a customary gift for kings.

The man illustrated is wearing a corselet of lamellar armour—this type of armour was introduced to the Middle East by the Turks, who probably wore these cuirasses instead of mail from the beginning of the crusades. Such cuirasses could be made of iron, horn or treated leather plates, and might open at the front or either side. The Seljuks wore such body armours right through the 12th and 13th centuries and under their influence the Arabs adopted it to a lesser degree, adding panels over, or set into, their mail hauberks. The Mamluks of the second half of the 13th century, being mostly Turks, also preferred the lamellar cuirass to a mail hauberk.

The bow case sometimes covered the entire bow and some warriors also carried their sword inside it. Note the knotted tail of the horse, a common practice amongst both the Turks and Arabs. This archer would also have carried a javelin.

G2 Mamluk askari, mid-13th century
This figure is wearing a lamellar cuirass beneath his robe, on the sleeves of which are embroidered bands (*tiraz*) bearing the honorific name or title of the wearer. On his head he wears the *bayda* (egg) helmet, a term which aptly describes this simple helmet, which was popular throughout the Islamic world, and which was often gilded or inlaid with an inscription from the Koran. The *bayda* could be worn on its own, or with a mail addition to the lower edges; the Mamluks from about mid-century onwards often protected the face by connecting the mail to the nasal so that only the eyes were uncovered. This last style was never adopted by the Arabs, and spread to the Middle East only through the influx of Turks in mid-century and through Persian influence on those Turks. It was also popular in Iberia.

The full-sized kite-shaped shield was used by the infantry of Egypt and Syria, but the mounted *askaris* used the smaller version illustrated here. The *askari* would also have carried a lance similar to that held by G3.

G3 Mamluk amir, second half 13th century
There were two main styles of mail armour worn by both the Mamluks and Arabs: the long coat or hauberk illustrated (usually with full length sleeves), and a short corselet with short sleeves, usually of thicker links. The amirs often wore the hauberk over the corselet for additional protection. The plate armour on the Mamluk's forearms is unusual before 1300.

The typical Mamluk sword, slung from a baldric, was reintroduced to Syria by the Mamluk sultans soon after mid-century. A round shield, slightly smaller than that shown in E3 and made of several layers of hide sewn together, is slung on the amir's back; he holds in his left hand a leather pouch, which was worn rather like a modern sabretache. Boots, such as those illustrated here and in G2, were the most common footwear, and were of leather or felt.

H1 Mamluk askari second half 13th century

Moslem nobles were more concerned with civilian fashion and appearance than their Frankish counterparts, and consequently their armour was usually hidden beneath a robe; the type of robe illustrated by figures H1, H2 and H3 indicated that the wearer was a military man. The mamluk illustrated here has the typical coat, boots, belt and arms of the 12th and 13th centuries, but the all-covering mail hood, over some other form of head defence, dates him to the second half of the 13th century; Seljuk head-dresses were frequently decorated with ribbons or peregrine falcon wings.

The stone glacis and main gateway of the massive Aleppo citadel. These parts were built in 1203–4 by the Ayyubid Malik az-Zahir; the remainder dates from *c.* 1292, when rebuilding was begun following the destruction of most of the citadel by the Mongols in 1260.

He also carries a small shield and would have a javelin. The quiver could hold 25–30 arrows.

H2 Syrian amir 12th–13th centuries

Another form of apparel, popular amongst Syrian amirs in the 12th century, was the brigandine, in which the knee-length mail hauberk was covered by a rich fabric (silk is shown here) and padded with linen waste. Sometimes the mail corselet formed an inner lining to such a coat. Such armour were very difficult to distinguish from civilian clothing (except for the wearer!), and the Frankish chroniclers of the crusades often failed to recognize the garments as armour, referring to the Saracen as being unarmoured. This type of body defence was not popular in Egypt until the Mamluks came to power. Mail hose are not shown in any known

Turkish or Saracen source.

The *bayda*, here with mail addition to protect the neck and face, was often worn over a small cap stuffed with feathers. In Syria the baldric was to some extent replaced in the 12th century by a sword belt round the waist, but both methods of sword suspension were used until about 1180, when the belt entirely replaced the baldric, except for the period 1193–1219 when the baldric was reinstated by the sultan. In the 12th century the amir was also armed with a lance about twelve feet long, with a slender diamond-shaped head.

H3 Mamluk askari 13th century

This figure is based on an illustration in a 13th century Mamluk military manual. Some form of body armour, probably a lamellar corselet, would have been worn under the coat. Other figures in the manual wear basically similar clothing, the coat occasionally having short sleeves and exposing the long sleeves of the undergarment. The javelin could be used as both a missile and a shock weapon, and the man would also carry his composite bow and a sword or a small axe or mace. The spurs are unusual; certainly the Seljuks and Arabs do not appear to have used them during the 12th and 13th centuries.

H4 Turkish archer 12th–13th centuries

Based on a figure on a 13th-century bowl found in Aleppo, this illustrates an auxiliary Turcoman mercenary such as served in most Islamic armies. He would have been mounted and probably wore a cuirass under his coat. The composite bow was about three feet long: the bows of the Arabs were about five feet in length. Damascus in particular was famous for its bows, and its bowmen: Aleppo was more noted for its infantry and miners.

H5 Turcoman auxiliary 12th–13th centuries

A mounted mercenary as H4, this figure wears a *bayda* beneath his turban and probably a lamellar corselet under his robe. The iron boss in the centre of his shield covers a simple horizontal grip, and his axe is of the small type favoured by some Turkish cavalrymen, instead of a sword, when in cavalry mêlée. The type of foot-gear illustrated appears both in early Seljuk sources and 13th-century manuscripts at Baghdad.

Chronology

1071 Byzantine army destroyed at Manzikert by Turks
1071–85 Seljuk Turks conquer Syria, Jerusalem and part of Palestine
1085 Toledo recaptured from Moors
1086 Spanish defeated at Zallaca

1096–99 1st Crusade

1097 Siege of Nicaea; battle of Dorylaeum; siege of Antioch
1098 Antioch captured; Edessa taken
1099 Jerusalem captured; battle of Ascalon
1101 Lombard, French and German forces, marching to reinforce army of Jerusalem, are destroyed by Turks; Arsuf and Caesarea taken by crusaders
1104 Acre captured; Franks of Antioch defeated at Harran
1109 Tripoli captured by crusaders
1110 Sidon captured by crusaders
1115 Seljuks defeated at Tell Danith
1119 Battle of the Field of Blood
1124 Tyre captured by crusaders
1137 Byzantine campaigns against Armenia and Antioch
1138 Byzantine emperor enters Antioch
1139 Moors defeated at Ourique by Alfonso VI
1142 Byzantines attack Antioch
1144 Zangi recaptures Edessa
1146 Almohades invade Spain

1147–48 2nd Crusade

1153 Ascalon taken by crusaders
1154 Damascus submits to Nur ed-Din
1158 Byzantium forces Antioch to submit
1163–9 Frankish campaigns against Egypt
1167 Shirkuh defeats allied armies of Egypt and Jerusalem
1169 Shirkuh occupies Cairo for Nur ed-Din: Saladin succeeds Shirkuh and deposes last Fatimid caliph
1174 Saladin takes Damascus
1176 Byzantine army destroyed by Turks at Myriocephalum
1183 Saladin takes Aleppo
1184 Almohades invasion of Spain defeated
1187 Franks defeated at Hattin; Jerusalem surrenders
1188 Saladin takes Saone and Kerak: Almohades invasion of Spain defeated.

1189–92 3rd Crusade

1190 Death of Frederick Barbarossa in Cilicia; surviving Germans arrive at siege of Acre
1191 Arrival of Philip of France and Richard of England at Acre; recapture of Acre; battle of Arsuf
1192 Battle of Jaffa; Almohades invade Portugal
1193 Death of Saladin
1195 Castilians annihilated by Moors at Alarcos

1202–4 4th Crusade

1203 Crusaders take Constantinople
1204 Crusaders retake Constantinople from new emperor and establish first Latin emperor
1212 Moors defeated at Las Navas de Tolosa by united Iberian armies

1218–21 5th Crusade

1219 Damietta captured but evacuated after two years

South façade of the northern enclosure of the citadel of Cairo. This part was built by Saladin, but the citadel was completed by his son and successor.

1228–9 6th Crusade

1229 Frederick II regains Jerusalem by treaty
1230 Teutonic Order establishes a base on Vistula
1233 Valencia taken by Jaime I of Aragon; first crusade launched against Prussian tribes
1236 Cordova taken by Fernando III of Castile

1239–40 Crusade of Theobald of Champagne

1240 Teutonic Order defeated at Liegnitz
1242 Prussian tribes revolt
1244 Jerusalem sacked by Khwarismians; crusaders defeated at Gaza
1247 Ascalon retaken by Egyptians

1248–54 7th Crusade

1249 Damietta taken by crusaders
1250 Battle of Mansourah; Louis defeated; Mamluks seize throne; Louis ransomed by surrender of Damietta
1254 German crusade launched to crush another Prussian revolt
1258 Mongols capture Baghdad
1260 Mongols take Aleppo and Damascus but

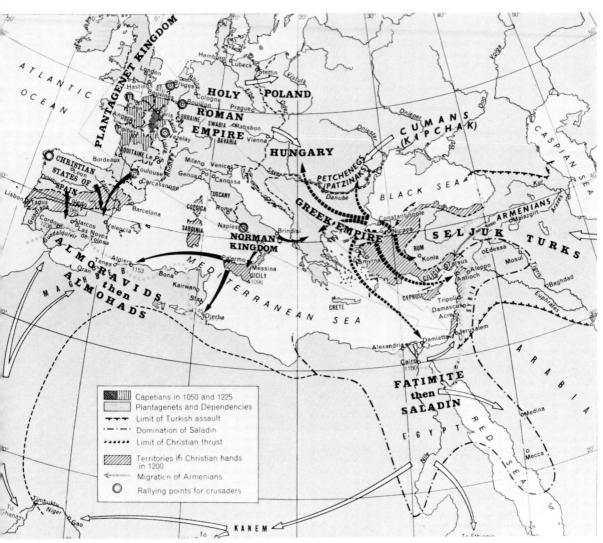

Movements of Christians and Moslems in the 12th century.
(Larousse)

Notes sur les planches en couleur

A1 Croisé 1er et 3e Croisades. Bien qu'un chevalier ne fut pas forcément noble qu'après sa première croisade, ce guerrier est de rang élevé et plus protégé de mailles que des croisés moins riches. Des hauberts à manches longues n'étaient la mode que jusqu'à la troisième croisade, mais ils n'ont jamais complètement supprimés la version à manches courtes. **A2** Un chevalier 3e croisade. En 1189 les manches du haubert ont été allongées pour former des mitaines; L'aventail à travers la partie inférieure de la figure fut introduit à la fin du 11e siècle et la protection des jambes étaient en usage courant par des chevaliers en 1150. **A3, A4** Des croisés 1er et 3e Croisades. Ceux-ci étaient des hommes de guerre plus pauvres et ressemblent à ceux depoints sur la tapisserie de Bayeux complétée en 1070–80. **A5, A6, A7** Des croisés du 12e siècle. Le surcot porté par le personnage A6 commençait à être à la mode à ce moment là; on pense que ce vêtement était copié des Sarassins et porté pour rendre le personnage plus élégant.

B1 Arbalétrier *c.* 1180–1300. L'arbalète était utilisée considérablement pendant la 1ère Croisade à la fin du 12e siècle un bâton composé et plus solide était utilisé. Les meilleurs arbalétriers venaient de Gênes et des Pays-Bas. **B2** Sergent *c.* 1220–13. A la terre sainte les sergents étaient habituellement des soldats armés, inférieurs en équipement et rang à des chevaliers, qui montaient en deuxième rang de cavalrie. **B3, B4** Des soldats d'infanterie *c.* 1200–1300. L'armure de corps en tissus était moins chère que la maille, et peut-être divisée en deux types principaux; l'aketon et le gabeson. Le premier modèle était fait de bougran et bourré de coton et piqué verticalement et le sécond était bourré de lin ou de lambeaux et piqué en carré ou carreaux. **B5** Frondeur 1100 à 1300. Le haut niveau de dextérité nécessaire pour utiliser cette arme étaient acquis d'habitude par des paysans qui n'avaient pas d'autre méthode pour défendre leur bétail.

C1 Chevalier *c.* 1225 à 60. Des changements importants ont eu lieu au 13e siècle quand le chevalier a voulu mieux se protéger. **C2** Chevalier *c.* 1250–1300. Deux nouveautés de cette époque étaient la division des mitaines en mailles en doigts séparés et l'introduction des défenses en métal pour le genou. **C3** Chevalier Hospitalier 1248–59. Le surcot noir était introduit en 1248, mais était remplacé par un rouge avec une croix blanche en 1259.

D1 Chevalier Teutonique *c.* 1230–83. Les campagnes Teutoniques contre les Prussiens étaient menées en plein hiver et les surcots blancs et manteaux devaient être un bon camouflage, bien qu'ils fussent introduits en 1191 à Outremer. **D2** Hochmeister de l'ordre Teutonique *c.* 1219. La bordure en argent autour de la croix était changée en or en 1219, lorsque le Roi de Jérusalem donna la permission de porter la croix en or sous celle en noir de l'Ordre. **D3** Schwertbrüder *c.* 1270 L'étendard pouvait également avoir deux épées croisées sous la croix allemande.

E1 Un noble espagnol début 13e siècle. Ce personnage est basé sur l'effigie sur le tombeau de Fernando de la Cerda au monastère de Las Huelgas près de Burgos. **E2** Chevalier espagnol au milieu du 13e siècle. Les manches jusqu'aux coudes du surcots le placent au milieu du siècle, autrement il a l'air d'être un ces chevaliers espagnols pendant tout ce siècle. **E3** Un soldat d'infanterie mauresque 12e siècle. Ce bouclier était typique à travers l'Islam; il était fabriqué de bois et gansé de cuir ou simplement poli. **E4** Cavalier Mauresque fin 12e siècle. Ce bouclier, fait de plusieurs couches de cuir durci cousues ensemble fut introduit en Espagne par les Berbères.

F1 Byzantine Peltast début du 12e siècle. Son armure piquée d'une façon épaisse et garnie de clous était sans doute faite par mesure d'économie et dû à la manque de fonds à cette époque. **F2** Officier de la garde Varangian, fin du 11e siècle. Ces gens étaient les plus loyaux de l'Armée et étaient surout des Anglo-Saxons qui s'étaient enfuis devant les invasions danoises. **F3** Cavalrie Byzantine fin 11e siècle. Parmi l'armée Byzantine chaque turma utilisa une couleur distinctive.

G1 Archer Seljuk à cheval au 12e siècle. Le manteau long, les nattes longues, collier et boucles d'oreilles sont tous typiques des Turques Seljuk. **G2** Mamluk askari milieu du 13e siècle. Le casque bayda était à la mode à travers le monde d'Islam, et pourrait être porté avec la maille protectrice pendante de chaque côté inférieur. **G3** Mamluk amir deuxième partie du 13e siècle. L'épée Mamluk typique fut introduite en Syrie par les Sultans Mamluks peu après 1250.

H1 Mamluk askari deuxième partie du 13e siècle. Les nobles Musulmans étaient plus préoccupés par des modes civiles que leurs analogues Francs, par conséquent leurs armures étaient souvent cachées sous des robes. **H2** Amir Syrien 12e et 13e siècles. L'haubert de maille à hauteur des genoux couvert d'un tissus somptueux, n'avaient pas l'air d'être de l'armure et souvent on pensait que les Sarassins n'étaient pas armés. **H3** Mamluk askari 13e siècle. Ses éperons sont insolites car ni les Seljuks ni les Arabes ne semblaient en avoir utilisés au 12e et 13e siècles. **H4** L'archer Turque 12e et 13e siècles. Ce personnage est basé sur un bowl du 13e siècle trouvé à Alep. **H5** Turcoman auxiliaire 12e et 13e siècles. Ce mercenaire à cheval porte un bayda sous son turban et sans doute un corselet lamellaire sous sa robe.

Farbtafeln

A1 Kreuzfahrer der 1.–2. Kreuzzüge. Dieser Krieger, vom hohen Stande, trägt umfangreichere Panzerrüstung als bei ärmeren Kreuzfahrer der Fall war. Langärmelige Kettenpanzerhemde waren vor dem 3. Kreuzzuge nicht in verbreitetem Gebrauch und haben die kurzärmeligen nie völlig ersetzt. **A2** Ritter des 3. Kreuzzuges. Bis 1189 hatten sich die Ärmel in Fäustlinge ausgedehnt; das Untergesicht schützende *aventail* wurde am Ende des 11. Jahrh. eingeführt und der Beinpanzer war schon gegen 1150 in allgemeinem Gebrauch. **A3, A4** Kreuzfahrer der 1.–3. Kreuzzüge. Diese waren ärmere Krieger und ähneln denen, die im Bayeux Wandteppich geschildert sind: der Wandteppich wurde 1070–80 fertiggestellt. **A5, A6, A7** Kreuzfahrer von der Mitte des 12. Jahrh. Der in Abb. A6 getragene Überrock kam zuerst um diese Zeit in verbreitetem Gebrauch; vermutlich wurde dieses Kleidungstück von den Sarazenen nachgeahmt.

B1 Armbrustschütze *c.* 1180–1300. Die Armbrust war im ersten Kreuzzug in weitem Gebrauch. Die geschicktesten Armbrustschützen stammten aus Genua und den Niederländern. **B2** Unteroffizier *c.* 1220–1300: ein gepanzerter Soldat er stand einem Ritter in Austüstung und Stande nach, und ritt in der zweite Reihe der Reiterei. **B3, B4** Fusssoldaten *c.* 1200–1300. Stoffene Körperschutzbekleidung war billiger als Kettenpanzer. Swei Hauptsorten waren *aketon* und *gambeson*. Die erste war aus mit Baumwolle gefüllem Steifleinen gemacht, und senkrecht gesteppt. Die zweite wurde mit Flachs oder Stofffetzen gefüllt und entweder in Vierecken oder Karos gesteppt. **B5** Schleuderer 1100–1300. Landmänner waren meistens mit der Schleuder sehr geschickt, da diese ihre einzige Waffe zum schützen ihre Viehs war.

C1 Ritter *c.* 1225–60. Grössere Änderungen traten im 13. Jahrh. ein, als der Ritter besseren Schutz suchte. **C2** Ritter 1250–1300. Die Abteilung der Kettenpanzerfäustlinge in getrennte Finger und die Plattenrüstung für den Knie besonders bemerken. **C3** Johanniterritter 1248–59. Der schwarze Überrock wurde im Jahre 1248 eingeführt, wurde, aber, in 1259 durch einen roten mit weissem Kreuz ersetzt.

D1 Deutschritter *c.* 1230–83. Die deutschen Feldzüge gegen die Preussen wurden in Hochwinter durchgeführt und die weissen Überröcke, obgleich diese im Jahr 1191 in Outremer eingeführt worden sind, müssen gute Schutzfärbung dargestellt haben. **D2** *Hochmeister* des Deutschordens *c.* 1219. Der Silberrand um das Kreuz wurde im Jahre 1919 in Gold gewandelt, da der König von Jerusalem dieses Recht vergönnt hatte. **D3** *Schwertbrüder c.* 1270. Die Fahne war manchmal auch durch gekreuzte Schwerter über einem deutschen Kreuz gekennzeichnet.

E1 Spanischer Edelmann Anfang des 13. Jahrh., dem Grabmale von Ferdinand de la Cerda in Las Huelgas nach. **E2** Spanischer Ritter der Mitte des 13. Jahrh. Die zum Ellenbogen reichenden Armel des Kettenpanzerhemdes deuten an die Mitte des Jahrhunderts: in anderen Beziehungen stellt er das Aussehe spanischer Ritter des ganzen Jahrhunderts dar. **E3** Mohrischer Fusssoldat des 12 Jahrh. Dieser Schild war durch die ganze Islamwelt typisch; der war aus Holz gemacht und entweder mit Leder bezogen oder einfach poliert. **E4** Mohrische Reiter am Ende des 12. Jahrh. Dieser aus verschiedenen zusammengenähte Lederschichten gebaute Schild wurde in Spanien von den Berbern eingeführt.

F1 *Byzantischer Peltast* am Anfang des 12. Jahrh. Gesteppte Polsterung anstatt Platenpanzer war wahrscheinlich aus Sparsamkeit im Gebrauch. **F2** Waragergar dist des späten 11. Jahrh. Dieser äusserst vertrauenswerte Teil des Heeres bestand aus Angelsachsen, die den dänischen Angriffen entflohen waren. **F3** Byzantische Reiter des späten 11. Jahrh. Innerhalb des byzantischen Heers trug jedes *turma* eine kennzeichnende Farbe.

G1 *Seljuk*, reitender Schütze des 12. Jahrh. Der lange Rock, die langen Zöpfe, der Halsband und die Ohrringe kennzeichnen alle die Seljuktürken. **G2** *Mamluk askari* von der Mitte des 13. Jahrh. Der *bayda*- War in verbreiteter Gebrauch durch die ganze Islamwelt und konnte mit von den Rändern abhängendem Kettenpanzerschutz getragen worden sein. *Mamluk amir* der zweiten Hälfte des 13. Jahrh. Der typische Mamelukschwert wurde in Syrie kurz nach 1250 eingeführt.

H1 *Mamluk askari* der zweiten Hälfte des 13. Jahrh. Muselmanische Edelmänne achteten mehr auf Zivilmoden als die entsprechende Franken und verbarge deshalb ihr Panzer unter einem Kleid. **H2** Syrischer *amir* 12.–13. Jahrh. Das den Knien reichende Kettenpanzerhemd war mit reichem Stoff überdeckt und sah nicht wie Panzer aus. Deshalb dachten Viele, dass die Sarazener keine Panzer trugen. **H3** *Mamluk askari* des 13. Jahrh. Seine Sporen sind aussergewöhnlich, denn weder die Seljuk noch die Arabier scheinen während der 12, und 13 Jahrh. Sporen gebraucht zu haben. **H4** Türkischer Schütze 12.–13. Jahrh. Diese Abbildung beruht auf eine in Aleppo gefundene Schale des 13. Jahrh. **H5** Turkmenischer Hilfssoldat des 13.–13. Jahrh. Dieser reitende Söldner trägt ein *bayda* unter seinem Helm und wahrscheinlich einen Brustharnisch aus Plattenpanzer unter seinem Kleid.